I0418734

Third Person

Notes On A First Year

Rachael Maddux

Vanitas Books

Copyright © 2025 by Rachael Maddux. All rights reserved.

No part of this book may be reproduced in any form or by any electronic or mechanical means, including information storage and retrieval systems, without written permission from the author, except for the use of brief quotations in a book review.

Cover design by Rachael Maddux. Cover image from *Mrs. Robert Shurlock (Henrietta Ann Jane Russell, 1775–1849) and Her Daughter Ann*, by John Russell (1801), from the Metropolitan Museum of Art's Open Access collection.

ISBN: 979-8-9923566-2-5 (paperback), 979-8-9923566-3-2 (ebook)

Contents

Preface

In October 2022, I had a baby. Between December 2022 and October 2023, I published the following essays through my newsletter, Vanitas. Several years earlier, I'd committed to sending one short personal piece every month, and although that pre-baby version of myself had a very different relationship to certain aspects of human existence —namely, time itself—I remained devoted, post-baby, to continuing the project. I was driven in part by stubbornness and in part by superstition. If I didn't keep writing, what would happen? I couldn't bear to find out.

And then the urgency broke like a fever. The baby had her first birthday, soon after that stopped breastfeeding, and soon after that started going to daycare. I responded to all this strange new freedom by giving up the newsletter entirely. I no longer required it keep my sense of self intact; I was also not sure I had anything left to say.

Another year passed, enough time to blur the rawness of those early days, enough time to get nostalgic. I found myself wishing I'd taken notes. I found myself wondering if I could write a book about having a baby. Then I realized, quite to my delight, that I *had* taken notes, I *had* written that book, or at least as much of that book as I would probably ever write.

"For now," I'm tempted to add to that sentence, the way I was apparently tempted—and unable to resist—adding it to many sentences in these pieces. I was embarrassed to notice that so long after the fact, but when I made small revisions to these hastily-typed products of my sleep-deprived mind, I decided to keep the tic. It's on theme, I think, with the collection itself and early motherhood as a whole: repetitive, more than a bit sloppy, aware of nothing if not the temporariness of every little thing.

Ding Dong
December 2022

This time last year was the saline ultrasound and the endometrial biopsy and the hysterosalpingogram, then the antibiotics, then the IVF orientation, then the follow-up biopsy, and all the while the hemming and hawing, the percentages and the dollar signs, the impossible calculations where n was a baby and x equaled WTF and y was well why not just try again on our own? Then there was Super Bowl Sunday and the *huh here we go again* feeling, then the creeping sick feeling, familiar then unfamiliar, steamroller fatigue, colors too loud, back molar barf button right where the toothbrush hit. Then one good appointment then another, the shadowy pictures they'd never printed for us before handed over like a CVS receipt and marveled at in the car while "Da Butt" played on the radio.

Now she's here, she's been here, and at various points over the last 10 weeks—despite everything, despite living through the years of her acutely not existing and the months of her existing more and more and more—I've found myself wondering about her life before she came to us, if this cry or that frown might stem from some obscure negative association with her previous owners. Like how, when we first got the dog from the shelter, a doorbell rang on TV and he popped up to stare at our front door. We marveled over it, this little flash of his life before. He knew a doorbell! Joe had the same thoughts about the baby. He told me like he was confessing something I'd think was really boneheaded but of course I just laughed. One day she'll talk about us to her friends and call us by our first names like we're exasperating coworkers or people in a book. We are the previous owners. We are the ones to blame.

"Have a baby??? Or be OK with not having a baby?????" was my resolution for so many New Years that it's weird going into January without all those question marks. There are plenty other questions this year (why IS she crying?). Some have ready answers, others don't need answers at all, and the rest I'm fine with leaving a mystery. At least for now.

The Babies In My Phone

January 2023

The baby in my house goes to sleep or maybe she doesn't and it's time to check in on the babies in my phone.

The babies in my phone were born a day before my baby, they were born last year and this year and yesterday. The babies in my phone are pink and brown and round and screaming. The babies in my phone are named after great aunts and baseball players and dead cats. The babies in my phone are rolling front to back. The babies in my phone are rolling back to front. The babies in my phone are sitting up. The babies in my phone are falling over. They are flailing and scooting and crawling. They are reaching for their fathers' beer bottles. They are sliding off couches. They are caught just in time.

The babies in my phone transmit their thoughts via letterboard. The babies in my phone say "HELLO WORLD!" The babies in my phone say "WORTH THE WAIT!" The babies in my phone are measured in weeks then months. "NINE IN, NINE OUT!"

The babies in my phone are meeting their big siblings. The babies in my phone are pulling the hair and violating the personal space of their big siblings. The babies in my phone are becoming big siblings. "PLOT TWIST!"

The babies in my phone are meeting the family dog, getting sniffed by the family dog, being guarded by one paw of the family dog, spooning with the family dog. The babies in my phone are *gentle pets, gentle, gentle*.

The babies in my phone are wearing shirts that say Mommy's Little Man and Daddy's Little Girl. The babies in my phone are correctly performing the gender announced via cupcake/balloon pop/fireworks display. The babies in my phone are wearing wool sweaters and linen overalls and hand sewn moccasins and turbans and sunglasses. The babies in my phone are engaging in age-appropriate play with aesthetically inoffensive wooden toys designed by a team of child development experts. The babies in my phone have a discount code for you. #ad #partner #letthembelittle

The babies in my phone look like Woody Harrelson and Clemenza from *The Godfather* and their own fathers and their grandfathers and anyone except the ones who birthed them.

The babies in my phone are sitting in a bucket.

The babies in my phone are laughing at their mothers peeling potatoes.

The babies in my phone could be a purple monkey in a bubblegum tree.

The babies in my phone have a deep latch, a shallow latch, they're milk drunk, they're sizing up, they're blowing out. The babies in my phone are eating kimchi for the first time. Pho for the first time. Lemons and they hate it. Hot Cheetos and they're unfazed.

The babies in my phone have stents and ports and GoFundMes. They are brave little warriors. They are small in large hospital beds. They are coming home. They have gone home to Jesus. They have memorial pages and foundations and 5K walk/runs.

The babies in my phone are getting hugged a little tighter tonight.

The babies in my phone are bad at napping but they sleep through the night.

The babies in my phone sleep through the night but they're bad at napping.

The babies in my phone are contact napping. Cat napping. Nap striking. Only in the carrier. Only in the stroller. Only in the swaddle. Arms out in the swaddle. Cold turkey on the swaddle. They are not sleeping. Not sleeping. Not sleeping. Not sleeping. They are sleeping but now they are regressing. They were regressing but now they're sleeping. Sleeping so long I thought they were dead, is that normal? Should I wake them up, is that normal?

They are drooling so much, is that normal?

Teething already, is that normal?

Pooping so much today, is that normal?

Haven't pooped today, is that normal?

Is 50th percentile, is that normal?

Seems to hate me, is that normal?

The babies in my phone are babes and bubs and bubbas and kiddos.

The babies in my phone have the sniffles today and this mama is soaking up alllllll the cuddles!

The babies in my phone got their shots today and they were fine but this mama's a mess!

The babies in my phone have their first Christmas in the books! First beach trip in the books! First day of daycare in the books! This mama's a mess!

The babies in my phone are suddenly all making "core memories."

The babies in my phone are getting so big. Big yawn!

Big stretch! They are chunks and chonks and chonkers. They are littles, they are these little loves. They will only be this little once, the babies in my phone.

The babies in my phone don't know they're in my phone.

The babies in my phone don't even know they're babies.

The babies in my phone mostly don't know me, except the ones who are wearing the clothes that will become my baby's hand-me-downs. My own baby, the baby in my house, the one who has been so many babies already, all of them already gone forever, all of them in my phone forever, the cloud forever, my heart forever. The one who is sleeping or maybe she isn't, the one who will smile when I wake her or maybe she'll cry. The one who is not just in my phone, she is my phone, she glows in the dark, she calls up the world.

Little Bum Bums
February 2023

I knew the baby was going to arrive on the cusp of an especially awful sick season, her rookie immune system no match for the quadruple-decker bus of cold and flu and RSV and COVID coming down the pike, and in theory I was more than fine with hiding her away until her six-month shots in the spring, but in reality I needed to leave the house.

Neighborhood walks had been our regular habit with the dog before he died last summer, then were neglected in his wake and in the cumbersome final stretch of my pregnancy, but once the baby was born they reemerged as a necessity, even with Joe and I and my pelvic floor all at our most exhausted. I needed the baby to see the world, I needed the world to see the baby, but I needed it too, even when, maybe especially when, my butt felt like it was going to fall out of my butt. Inside I was all rearranged, but outside everything—houses, dog park, Civil War battle plaques, soccer fields, confounding mixed-use redevelopment of former industrial blight, condos, churches, elementary school—was more or less where we left it.

Now, four months in, my body and soul are no longer in

such acute shambles and the baby's systems are generally more robust, but the walks are still very important. Half the time she falls asleep in her carrier but when she's awake she is *awake*, ooh-ing and ahh-ing, eyes wide, taking in everything and knowing nearly nothing about any of it, the world piecing itself together inside her cantaloupe head.

One afternoon earlier this month, on our way down the sidewalk by the elementary school, we came upon a guy in deep athleisure walking a very small dog. He was trying to tug her along but she saw us coming and dug in, legs making four little 45 degree angles to the ground. "Stubborn!" I said, and the guy said, "Oh yeah, she's gotta meet everybody." I bent down to oblige her. She barely cleared the top of my boots. Joe crouched and opened one side of the carrier so the baby could see. The baby looked around at everything except the dog. "What is this creature's name?" I asked, and the guy said, "Her name is Little Bum Bums." I gasped. I had so many questions, but the baby was beginning to fuss. Okay, okay, time to go.

All the way home I kept saying, "Little Bum Bums!" and for days I was telling everyone about how we met a dog named Little Bum Bums, and every time we walked past that spot on the sidewalk by the elementary school I said, "This is where we met Little Bum Bums. I will always remember that this is where we met Little Bum Bums." And Joe was like, "Yep, Little Bum Bums." And the baby was like, "Ah-goo."

One afternoon a week later, on our way down the sidewalk by the elementary school again, we found ourselves behind two women pushing toddlers in strollers. We were hanging back, trying not to crowd them, but I was getting itchy. The sidewalk was wide and they were side by side, taking up every inch of it, and they were going slow, so slow I thought Joe and I might fall over, so slow it was like we were walking backwards. I was trying to calculate whether it would be worth it to peel off and loop through the parking lot then scoot out ahead of them, or if we'd end up where we started, stuck sauntering all the way to the corner. Then came the car. It was not going slow, it was going fast, very fast, too fast in the wrong direction. It whooshed through my periphery, some kind of brown midsize SUV, swerved down the center line, then slammed to a stop to block the path of a black Land Rover. The brown SUV driver jumped out, yelling: "You hit my hand!" or "You hit my head!" and "You motherfucker!" and "You piece of shit!" and "You motherfucking piece of shit!"—over and over, rhythmic, captivating. The Land Rover just sat there, tinted windows impassive, a line of cars backing up on the street behind it.

Joe and I stopped, and the stroller women stopped, and we all stood there on the sidewalk, gaping at the scene. The brown SUV driver, possessed of the eloquence of the truly enraged, continued to yell as he threw open his back hatch, yelled as he reached in, yelled as he rummaged around under a pile of stuff. I could think of only one thing an angry man would be searching for in the back of his car while yelling at the car he'd cut off by speeding a block in the opposite lane. A gun, of course it was a gun.

Joe and the stroller women seemed to have the same thought at the same time. Suddenly we were moving again, not running but slowly piloting ourselves and our children away from the street and into the school parking lot. Where were we going? Where were we supposed to go? There was a car in the parking lot and I thought, *Hide behind the car. The car will keep you safe from what's happening.* But what was happening? The man, still yelling, had found what he was looking for and was now slamming it against the Land Rover's driver side window. The window shimmered a little with every blow.

It was a gun, but if it was a gun, why wasn't he shooting it? Joe and I stood behind the car in the parking lot, not quite committing to a full crouch. I thought of the talk radio DJ in my hometown who road-raged at a guy with a hatchet but the other guy had a gun and shot the hatchet-wielding talk radio DJ. I thought of the road-rage shooting in Midtown and the road-rage shooting in Brookhaven and the road-rage shooting on 285 and the road-rage shooting on 20 and Georgia's permitless concealed carry law and I thought, *If this guy doesn't have a gun, the other guy does*.

And I thought, *Hiding behind this car isn't going to do shit*.

The stroller women seemed to have already realized this. A maintenance building sat like a red brick island in the parking lot, bigger than the car, bigger than two stacks of cars, and they were headed towards it. I turned from the car to follow them. A few paces out, I looked over at Joe. He wasn't next to me. He was still behind the car, surveying the scene up on the street, the baby still strapped to his chest. *The baby*. Her cantaloupe head. He didn't know the car wouldn't save them. I felt a black hole opening up in my chest. I hissed his name and bugged out my eyes: *Get over here!* He moved one hand slightly: *No, it's okay*.

I looked up and saw he was right. The yelling man was no longer yelling and no longer pounding the gun or not-gun against the Land Rover's window. He was jumping back into his brown midsize SUV and driving away. His back hatch was still open. Stuff spilled into the street. The Land Rover was somehow already gone.

The stroller women emerged from the far side of the maintenance building, wheeling their toddlers towards us. One of them was very pregnant and the other was our neighbor whose husband gave us a stack of their daughter's board books after we had the baby.

"Are y'all okay?" someone walking their dog called across the parking lot.

"Oh sure, yeah!" our neighbor called back, laughing, something about collective trauma something something.

Part of my brain was still half a block back, trying to figure out how to politely skirt around these women and their contraptions, but now we were circling up in the parking lot and trading introductions like we'd all marked the date on our Google Calendars weeks ago. How sweet, how old is she? Could you tell what he was yelling? When are you due? Could you see what was in his hand? Sixteen weeks, no, next week, no, could you? We were all behaving quite nonplussed (informal definition) while I, for one, was feeling quite nonplussed (traditional definition). The toddlers gaped up at us. The baby grunted in her carrier and opened an eye. She'd been asleep the whole time.

"Do you think he'll come back for it?" the pregnant woman asked, and we all looked up at the stuff that had fallen out into the street. A series of cars thoroughly flattened a bottle of motor oil. A lady walking her dog waited for a pause in traffic then scurried out to retrieve a bigger hunk of plastic, set it on the curb, then went along her way. It was a booster seat, the kind for kids too big for a car seat but too small to ride unsupported, the kind that did not exist during our childhoods. Too many kids were dying in car accidents, apparently, so someone did something about it. A strange thing to ponder while standing in the parking lot of the elementary school where my daughter will one day learn how to hide from men with guns, just like I did once upon a time, for all the good it's done me.

Later, once we were home, Joe and I would wonder if the yelling man had a wife and what she would say, and what he would say, the next time she looked in the car for the booster seat.

Later, I would remember he was wearing a blue jersey—a coach from the soccer fields up the street, maybe. Joe would say the midsize SUV wasn't brown. He didn't know what color he thought it was but it wasn't brown.

Later, I would catch myself: wait, what did I think was going to happen? Like, the guy was going to shoot at the Land Rover and then...? Why did I think we were in danger? Well, why not?

Later, I would cry because I thought we were going to die back there, and then I would cry because I knew now I would always remember that spot on the sidewalk was somewhere I thought we were going to die, and then I would cry (I was just generally crying now) because that spot on the sidewalk was where we'd met Little Bum Bums, it was supposed to be where I remembered meeting Little Bum Bums, how dare this man's rage usurp something so pure as my memory of meeting Little Bum Bums?

And then I would think: I wanted to show the baby the world, didn't I? Well, so, what is the world if not the spot on the sidewalk, so to speak, where you meet a Little Bum Bums one day and fear for your family's life the next—all that and everything else, too—a pin dropped at the universal coordinates of terror and joy?

But that was all later. For now we just stood around the parking lot with the stroller women, chit-chatting our cortisol levels back to earth as the daylight faded into a warm, weird night, until the toddlers got squirmy and the baby began to fuss. Okay, okay, time to go.

Goodnight Nobody
June 2023

The baby slept in our bedroom for the first one hundred and ninety three nights of her life. Night one home from the hospital, Joe and I put her in a bassinet at the foot of our bed and none of us particularly enjoyed ourselves; night two, flying high on our pediatrician's blessing to co-sleep if we weren't drunk or high or swimming in blankets, we put her between us, a wiggly comma between the anxious parentheses of our bodies; night three, catastrophically cricked and no better rested, we finally mustered the sliver of brain power required to try and set up our Snoo. We stationed it against the wall four steps from my side of the bed—an obscene distance, I thought, for someone who'd slept inside my body for most of the previous forty weeks. But she liked it fine, so there she stayed. It was a generous hand-me-down and we never figured out how to connect it to our Wi-Fi network or to the app, but we swaddled and clipped her in every night anyway, like a little grub blasting off to outer space.

Still, nearly every night for weeks afterwards I woke up thinking the baby was in the bed with us: wadded up in the comforter or smothered between our pillows or crushed underneath me. I would wake up gasping and paw around madly until Joe woke up too and assured me that she was fine—or she would remind me herself, over there in the Snoo, with a whimper or a whinny or a fart—and then I would collapse with relief and sometimes even get myself back to sleep before the next time she woke under her own great delusion (that she'd never been fed in her long, long life).

At that point, to be awoken by anything except the baby herself felt like a great act of violence, and my relief at her safety was always tinged with regret. If only if only *if only* we hadn't put her in our bed that one night, if only I hadn't given my dumb greedy subconscious access to a true memory it could spin into a mean little middle-of-the-night lie! But then I realized it probably didn't matter, actually, because this is just something my brain does, with or without my help.

I have one mushy memory of what might be my first sleep hallucination—laying in bed in my family's old house, staring at a doll on my bookshelf, watching her mouth move and straining to hear what she was saying—but then again, my childhood was kind of one big mirage that toys were talking to me, so not sure if that counts. The first I can be sure was a true hallucination happened when I was maybe eleven. I fell asleep on my cousin Marie's bottom bunk with her family's elderly cat curled at my feet, woke with the absolute certainty that I'd kicked the cat and killed it, then watched as its ghost rose up from the bed and floated away. I came to in a panic, woke up Marie, made her go find the cat (the cat was fine) and then made her switch bunks with me in case the ghost of the non-dead cat came back for me (it never did). There must have been others in my teenaged years and in college, but I recall only a peak in my early twenties when I first lived alone: rats swinging on mini-blind cords, a black dog running through my studio apartment, the shadow of a man in a wide-brimmed hat standing motionless at the foot of my bed. Each of them as real as real could be until something in my head popped like a bubble and I found myself sitting up alone and panting in a quiet, gray-dark room.

I Googled my way to a name: They're hypnagogic when they happen on the way into sleep and hypnopompic when they happen on the way out. They're not dreams, not exactly night terrors, more like a weird misprojection from my brain onto the scrim of whatever that falls and rises between asleep and awake. That helped a little, knowing that I wasn't imagining that I was imagining something—that the unreality was real in its own way.

But they tend to feel real in the real way, too. That's the thing, and I don't think I realized *how* real until Joe and I moved in together, more than a dozen years ago now, and all of a sudden I had an audience. I would wake up and Joe would wake up because I woke up—either because I sat up so abruptly he thought something was wrong, or because I screamed; I had no idea, until he told me, that sometimes I screamed. Once he clocked that neither of us were being murdered, he would gently inform me that I was having a sleep hallucination. (He used to say just that: "You're having a sleep hallucination." Now he just says, "Sleep 'lucie, babe.") After arguing with him— absolutely insistent that our dog was sitting on top of the dresser, or that someone was having a big party in the backyard, or that there was blood dripping down the wall—the bubble would pop and I would say, "Oh," and flop back to sleep. He reports, even now, that I always sound disappointed when I realize I'm wrong and there's truly nothing there.

So then came the baby. Mostly she was lost in the bed. But one night she was starfished on the ceiling above us, one night she was nestled in the junk basket under my night-stand, one night she was bobbing upside down in my water bottle. My waking hours were simultaneously more and less real than they ever had, my sleeping hours were more fragile than ever, so I was extra unsure what to make of this in-between. Seeing her in all of these strange places was very alarming but also bemusing: *She barely knows she has hands, how did she open that lid?* I tried to remember to remind myself to look at the Snoo light for proof that she was where she was supposed to be. (If the light's blue, she's in the Snoo!) This worked, except for the non-zero number of times I put her in the Snoo and forgot to turn it on. (If the light's white, things ain't right.) And then those four steps never felt longer. But she was always there, right where we left her.

For the first five or so months, I thought about our nights with the baby in terms of how many times she woke us up. Around six months, though, I began to suspect it was becoming more of a team project. Her fun-sized farts occasionally roused me; what were ours doing to her? I was often unsettled by her tendency to emit a single piercing, desperate shriek for no apparent reason; what did she make of all my hollering at her hypno-doppelgangers? More than once I heard her crying and sprang out of bed and scrabbled around in the darkness for her pacifier only to realize it was still in her mouth—she hadn't chucked it, hadn't cried, only now she was, now she was pissed, now it was real.

So we moved her into a crib in her own bedroom. Another obscene distance, I thought, until my hunch was proven exactly right. We're all sleeping much better. I still wake up thinking she's lost in the blanket, or curled in the pile of laundry, or stuck inside the picture frame on the wall, but she doesn't have to hear me carrying on about it or her dad talking me back to reality, as I suspect he will be doing for the rest of our natural lives together. I can't see any sort of future where I don't worry, just a little bit, all the time, waking and sleeping, that this child isn't safe and breathing and exactly where she's supposed to be. For now, at least, I have a video monitor to check. Sometimes I do see strange faces in the rumple of her sleep-sack, and sometimes the flowers on her crib sheet crawl like fingers and bugs. But mostly I just see her: luminous even in grainy night vision, unclipped and unswaddled, sprawled face-down, my little grub out on her spacewalk, falling and falling and never hitting the ground.

Slice of Life
August 2023

In the beginning, the baby's nails were so delicate I could just pick them off when they got too long, like peeling off a bit of tape stuck to a gift. When they firmed up I attempted scissors exactly once (terrifying) then moved on to using one of the tiny emery boards that came in a "baby grooming kit" we acquired somehow, the contents of which was all so miniature it was like they expected the baby to be grooming herself. An adult-woman-sized nail file was easier to maneuver but also more easily grabbed; I did my best but somehow wound up sharpening her nails at least as often as I blunted them. More advanced technology was necessary. So I bought an electric buffer thingy, which soon became known as "the nail gun" when I couldn't remember "buffer thingy," and I deployed the accursed screen time.

For a while my one opinion on this subject was that most media for little kids looks and sound ghastly and I wanted to keep it out of my life for as long as possible, but otherwise, whatever, what's the big deal? But then I had a baby and the baby became... aware. If it glows, she stares. She is amused by the numbers on the washing machine;

faces moving and talking on television send her into an ecstatic trance. Her eyes become wide and blank. If her body is moved away from the screen, her head swivels as if magnetized to it. Part of me always wants to whisk her away to a sunlit room full of hand-whittled wooden toys, and another part of me feels like I should give her some privacy, like I'm crashing her very successful first date with the new love of her life. Now my opinion is this: One day I want my child to enjoy watching movies and TV as much as I do—these are true fonts of joy in life, necessary respites from and portals back into the world!—but I want her to engage with that world in a three-dimensional way as often as possible for as long as possible before the pixels have their way with her. This seems fair? But also, she was slicing the *hell* out of that three dimensional world, in particular her face, my face, and my boobs. So I thought, well, I guess *Our Planet* seems chill.

And it was, for like the first ten minutes of episode one. The baby sat in my lap, hypnotized, while I ground away at her petite claws. "One day you'll think it's funny that those birds are called boobies," I told her. No response; she was fully Attenborough-pilled. Next time, we picked up where we left off and, oops, here comes the thirsty baby flamingo tromping across the African salt pan, salt collecting on its feet in tragic little boots. And here are the wild dogs and the wildebeest calf. And here's a collapsing glacier. She began to wiggle and flap. "Yeah, kind of a bummer, huh, babe?" I said, but she was unmoved by the tragedy and majesty of nature; she was just bored.

New plan! We went high-contrast. Old black-and-white Roger Corman movies on YouTube did the trick for a while, bits and pieces of *Attack of the Crab Monsters* and *Not Of This Earth*. Then more wiggling and flapping. Onto vintage *Sesame Street*! She grooved on the theme song, but when Big Bird showed up she looked over her shoulder at me like, *What the hell is this?* "Acquired taste, maybe?" I said to excuse the most beloved TV show of all time. She grabbed the nail gun and shoved its spinning tip into her mouth, talons intact.

Next I suppose we could've escalated to Elmo, or even tried *Pee-Wee's Playhouse*, but at the time I thought: Enough. Done with chill, done with cool, done with nostalgia. Time for the hard shit.

I don't even know how I came to know about Ms. Rachel. It was like I gave birth and suddenly there she was in my brain. She's a forty-something-year-old white lady who sings songs and does language development exercises for little kids on her YouTube channel. She has a bright, happy face and a bright, happy voice and a bright, happy uniform: pink headband, pink t-shirt, blue denim overalls. Somehow, before I ever saw a single one of her videos, I saw videos of little kids watching her videos, and they were utterly rapt, like it was Baby Videodrome. Meanwhile, my own child's eyes turn into big pulsing hearts at the sight of a Target self-checkout screen. I wasn't sure I wanted to see her see Ms. Rachel. But her fingernails were dirty as a coal miner's and my boobs looked like I'd been nursing a raccoon. I needed help.

"Okay, we're going in," I told the baby a few weeks ago. We settled onto the couch with the nail gun and I hit play on the first Ms. Rachel video YouTube served me. A mistake —it was a crossover episode with Blippi and Meekah. Somehow I already knew who Blippi was, too, and could guess that Meekah was part of his extended cinematic universe, though this knowledge did nothing to dull the sensation of my soul being roughly caressed by a microplane. "This is hell," said Joe, passing through the living room. "We are in hell." But the baby sat on my lap, still as a doll, elbows out, hands raised in surrender. She let me do a first pass on her nails, then a second, then her toes. I got in there so good I thought maybe I'd never have to do them again. I was wrong, of course, so a few days later it was back to Ms. Rachel—straight up, no Blippi, something called "Baby Learning 2," as if any video on YouTube wouldn't teach a baby something, but I was done making fun soon as this dear sweet woman appeared on the screen and said, "Hi! Hello! Can you say Mama? MA-ma! MA-ma!" and I could feel my child become ensorcelled.

So this is what we do now. Every few days we give ourselves over to Ms. Rachel. I hit play and this angel in a pink headband blasts us with her megawatt cheer, singing with puppets and dancing with cartoon animals, enunciating like a maniac, commanding and applauding her unseen infant army. (Joe leaves the room, bless his heart.) When I hit stop, the baby emerges from her stupor with her talons dulled once more and looks up at me like, *Wait, who are you again?* Maybe one day I'll tell her about the dream I had where I realized I was out in public dressed like Ms. Rachel, and later in the dream realized I was *becoming* Ms. Rachel. "You know, my name is Ms. Rachel too, kind of," I told her the other day. But she just lunged for the nail gun, totally unimpressed by her mother's selfhood, just as she's meant to be.

The Night Before
October 2023

The night before, I installed the wall-mount dock for the vacuum cleaner, and Joe made cheese-burgers, and we watched *The Horror of Dracula*. We said, let's go to breakfast in the morning then figure out the car seat. We went to bed.

That was Friday. I was due the following Monday, but had set my sights a week and a half later, forty-one and a half weeks, which I'd read was the average delivery date for first babies. She was going to be a Scorpio, like me, I was sure of it. I don't care much about astrology but I like being a Scorpio; people who do care say *oooh* when they find out, like it's not only meaningful information but surprising somehow, a little stinger.

Instead I woke up at 3am to vague bodily annoyance. Cramps? *Ugh my period's coming,* I thought, forgetting everything. Then remembering.

We did not go to breakfast. Joe threw the car seat into the back of the Prius when we left for the hospital in the last black moments of night. By 3pm I had gone out into the cosmos and turned inside out and she was in my arms, pink and chirping, expressive divots where her eyebrows would be. She kept throwing her arms into the air then lowering them slowly, like she was trying to catch her balance. A Libra, just under the wire.

Weeks later, back home, our doulas came to visit. They folded laundry and told me about the other babies they'd delivered that fall, how different they all were. They'd just visited one who, they agreed, had an old, wise soul. "What about this one?" I asked, and they studied her. "Cool, clear water," one of them said. "Yeah, I feel blues and purples," said the other. "Not an old soul?" I said. "No," they agreed, "she's never been here before."

For a year, every day that was true: *She's never been here before*. Next year is a leap year, so today isn't quite her last first day. But tomorrow begins her second orbit, her second spin through the stars. I'd like to be sleeping more. I'd like to be writing more. I think I left part of myself out there when I went to go get her. But give me a hundred more years with her, a hundred more lifetimes, it doesn't matter, it will never be enough.

Acknowledgments

Thank you to Abby Greenbaum, Hannah Palmer, and Laura McKee for the wisdom.

Thank you to Duvall Osteen for the support.

Thank you to Mindy Middleton, Dr. Heather Hipp, Dr. Sara Campbell, Lauren Bernazza, and Dr. Emily Kanaan for the care.

Thank you to the Madduxes, the Landises, and the McCormicks for the love.

And of course Joe, and of course Ramona, for everything.

About the Author

Rachael Maddux is a writer and editor. Her work has appeared in *Oxford American*, *Virginia Quarterly Review*, *The Believer*, and elsewhere. After many years in Atlanta, Georgia, she now lives with her family in Chattanooga, Tennessee, where she grew up.

For more, visit rachaelmaddux.com.

www.ingramcontent.com/pod-product-compliance
Lightning Source LLC
Chambersburg PA
CBHW020814130626
46554CB00006B/2435